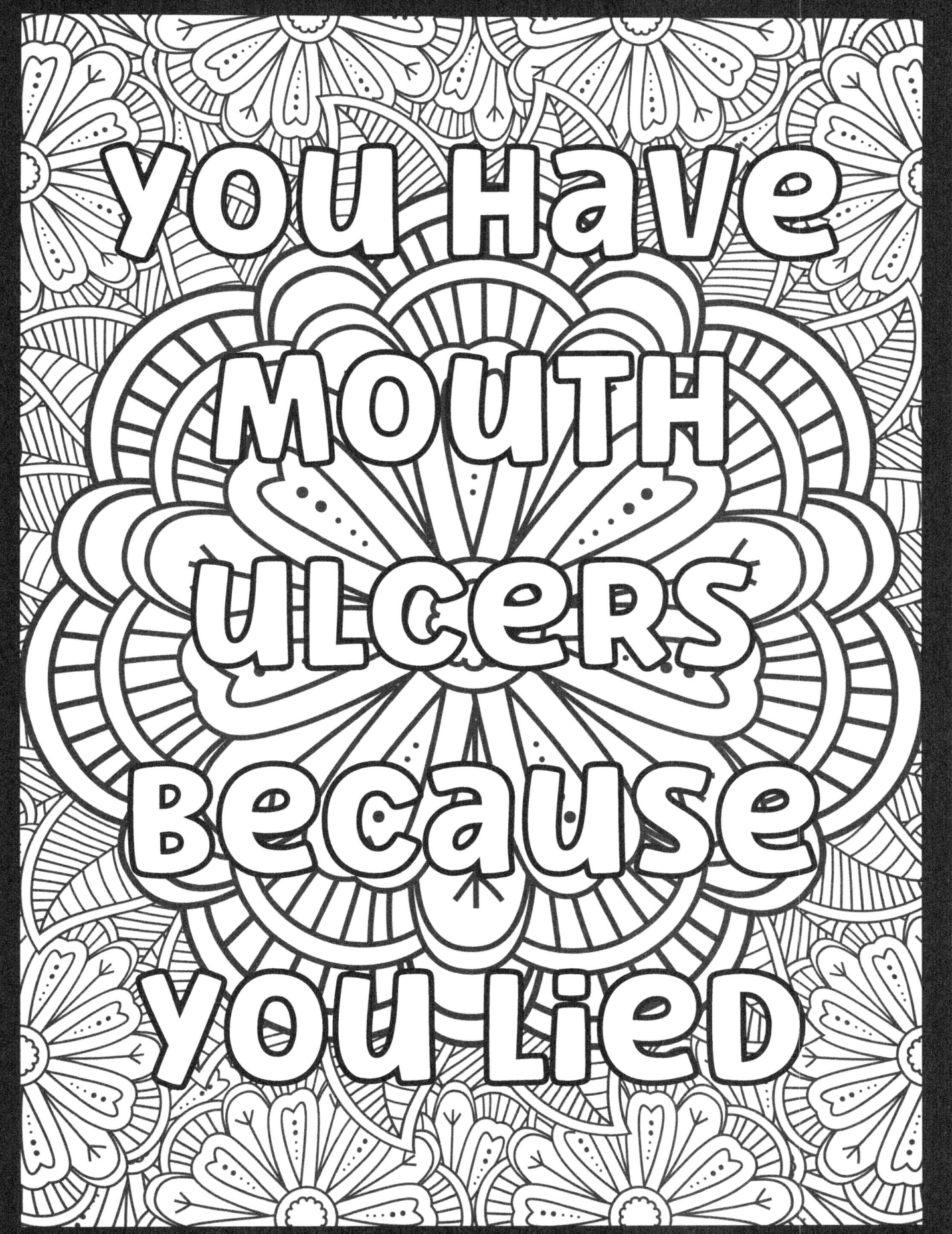

EAT YOUR CARROTS, THEY'LL HELP YOU SEE IN THE DARK

IF YOU PICK DANDELIONS YOU WILL WET THE BED

IF YOU SWALLOW APPLE PIPS A TREE WILL GROW IN YOUR STOMACH

The ice cream van plays music when its out of ice cream

THE DOG HAS GONE TO LIVE ON A FARM

if you wee in the swimming pool the water turns purple

CHOCOLATE MILK COMES FROM BROWN COWS

IF YOU SWALLOW YOUR GUM, IT WILL TAKE 7 YEARS TO DIGEST

THEY DON'T MAKE BATTERIES FOR THAT TOY ANYMORE

If you sneeze with your eyes open, they'll pop out

IF YOU DON'T TAKE A BATH, MOSS WILL GROW BEHIND YOUR EARS

IF YOU KEEP PLAYING WITH YOURSELF, YOU WILL GO BLIND

IF YOU KEEP CRACKING YOUR KNUCKLES YOU'LL GET ARTHRITIS

IT'S ILLEGAL TO HAVE THE LIGHT ON INSIDE THE CAR

IF YOU EAT THE CRUSTS ON YOUR TOAST, YOUR HAIR WILL GO CURLY

IF YOU DON'T CLEAN YOUR EARS, POTATOES WILL GROW THERE

IF YOU SIT ON COLD CONCRETE, YOU WILL GET PILES

IF YOU DON'T GET OUT THE BATH, YOU'LL BE SUCKED DOWN THE PLUG HOLE

If you tell lies, your tongue goes blue, stick out your tongue

THE TOOTH FAIRY ONLY VISITS CLEAN BEDROOMS

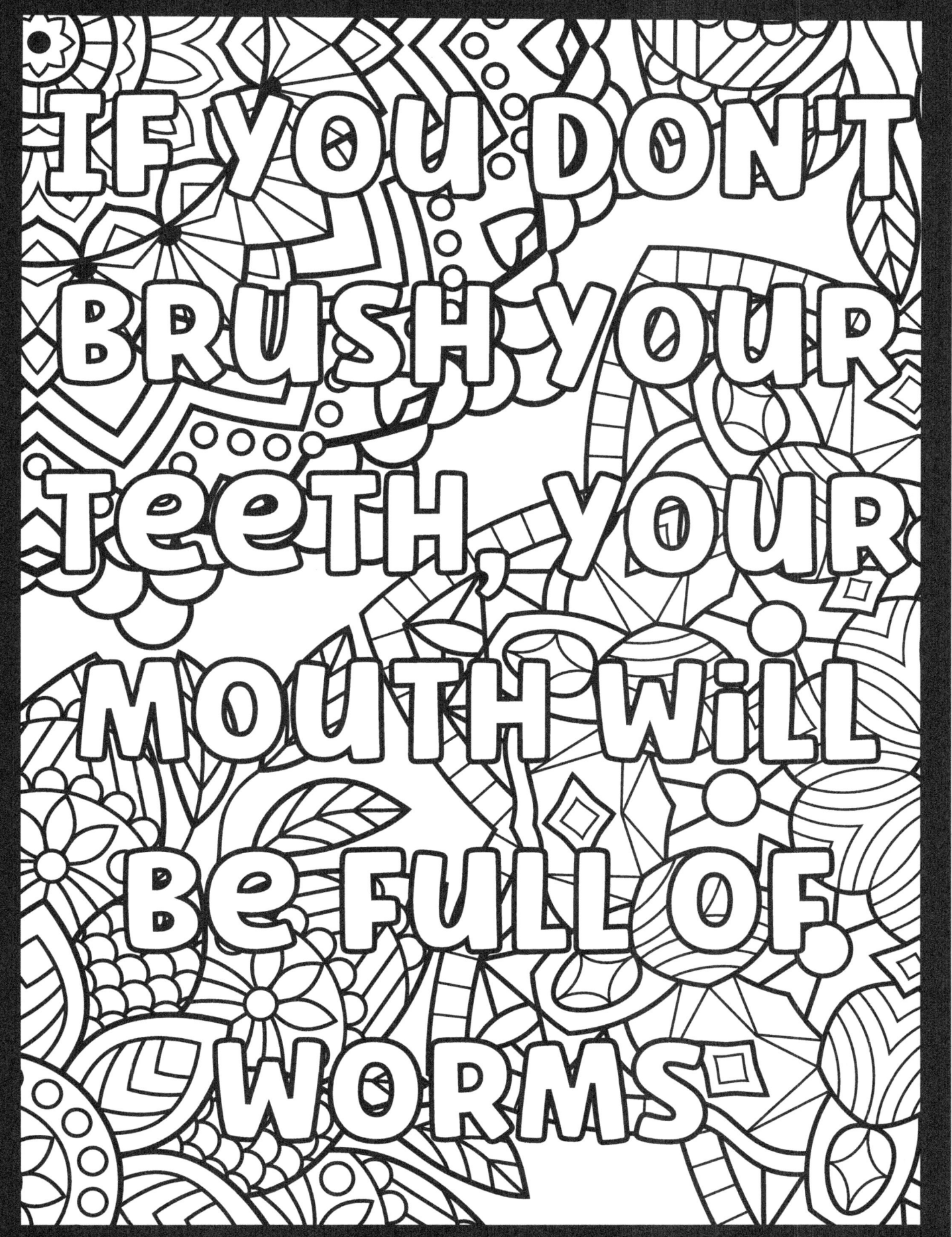

IF YOU LEAVE THE FRIDGE DOOR OPEN, PENGUINS DIE

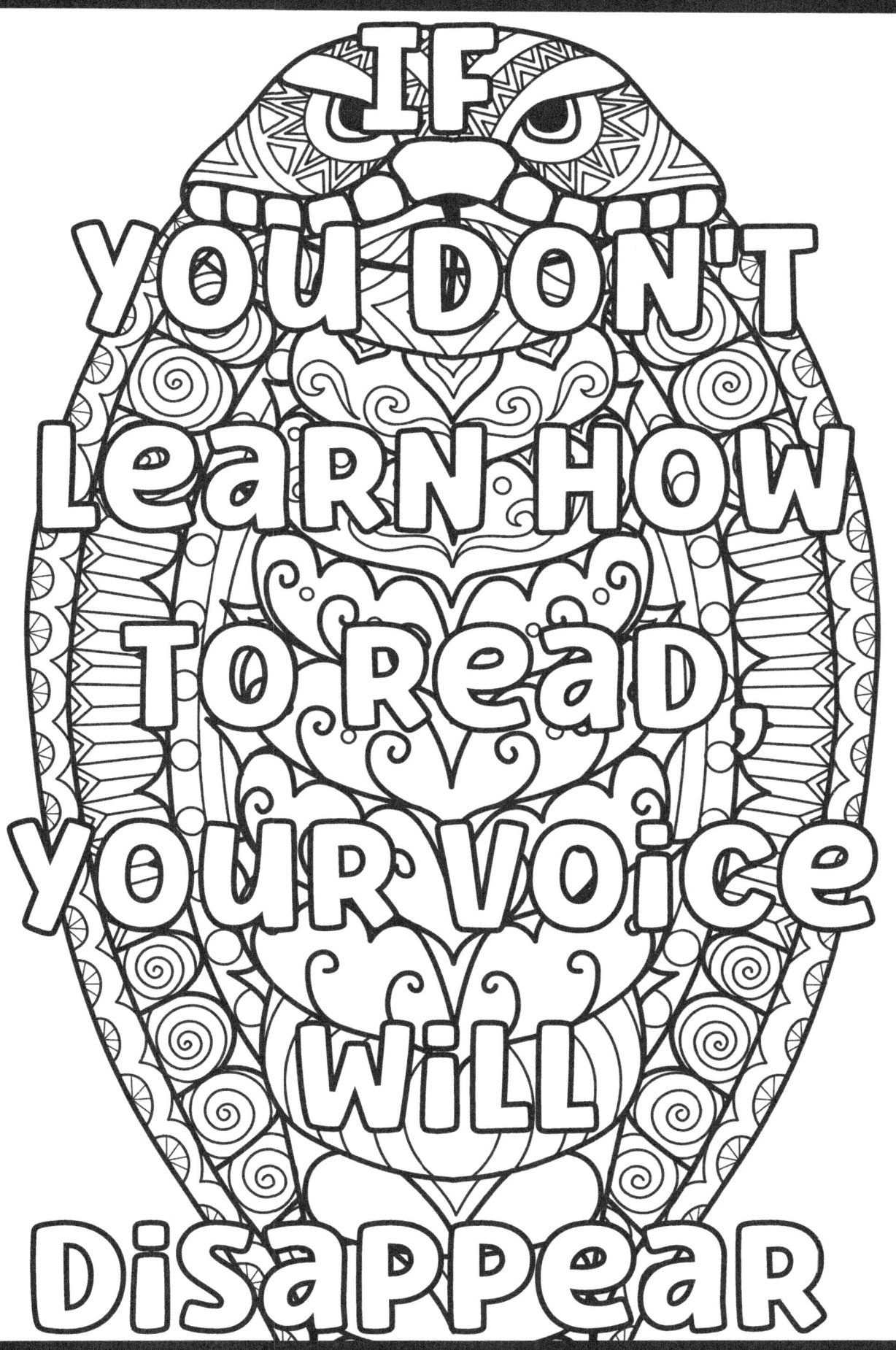

IF YOU BURP, FART AND SNEEZE AT THE SAME TIME, YOU TURN INSIDE OUT

IF YOU PLAY WITH YOUR WILLY, IT WILL DROP OFF

If you eat enough vegetables, your body makes them taste like candy

IF YOU EAT YOUR SPINACH, YOU'LL GET MUSCLES LIKE POPEYE

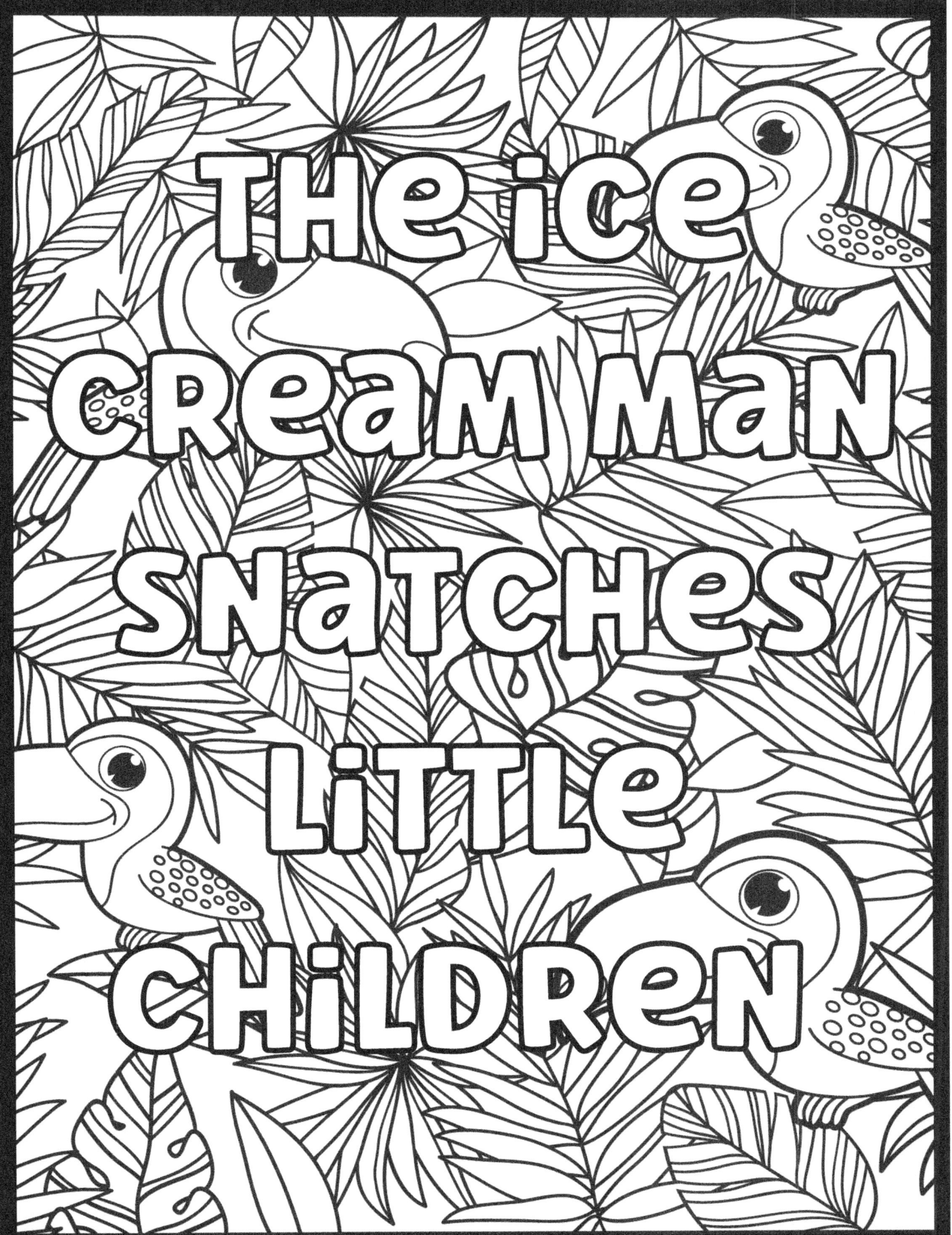

IF YOU READ IN THE DARK, YOU WILL GO BLIND

CLICK YOUR FINGERS TO MAKE THE TRAFFIC LIGHTS GO GREEN

I HOPE YOU ENJOYED YOUR TRIP DOWN MEMORY LANE

IF YOU LIKED THE COLORING BOOK, PLEASE CAN I ASK FOR YOU TO RATE IT ON AMAZON

Printed in Great Britain
by Amazon